MAKE A NOTE

WHAT YOU <u>REALLY</u> NEED TO KNOW ABOUT TEACHING ELEMENTARY MUSIC

JESSICA PERESTA

"Jessica Peresta's "Make A Note" is a great book for teachers who are at a new point in their teaching career, whether it's as a brand new teacher, a teacher switching to a new school, or a teacher changing levels. Her positivity and honesty draw the reader in, helping them to find ways to prioritize their lives (and those to-do lists!), take care of themselves and all of their relationships, and be the best music teacher that they can be. Jessica acknowledges that every teacher is different, and what works for her might not work for any other teacher. She encourages her reader to find out what will make them successful, and then put all of the pieces into place so that they can be an excellent music teacher. Jessica talks about how it can be difficult, especially if you are the only music teacher in your school. The emphasis on the importance of relationships - family, friends, coworkers, and students - makes it clear that Jessica was a successful teacher, and wants each reader of her book to feel the same way."

Amy Johnson

"Jessica has done a terrific job of portraying the real-life young teacher and all of the joys and tribulations that go along with the day-to-day life in a music classroom. She succinctly discusses every little nuance and the many possible resolutions and does it with a humorous tone. So easily relatable, even for "seasoned" teachers. A great read!"

Wendi Rounce

"Make A Note" is a must-read for first-year music teachers! I wish I could have read this book before my first year, but it is a great tool for any music teacher. It was as if Jessica was talking directly to me and knew how I was feeling. This book is easy to read and will be one that I reread every year."

Jenifer Phillips

"I wish "Make A Note" had been available to me before my first year of teaching! Jessica's book should be required reading for every college Music Education major and student teacher. This book goes into every nitty-gritty detail of the life of an elementary music teacher. Jessica shares her story and experiences teaching elementary music in such a honest, warm way. It feels like a mentor teacher and their mentee talking about their school week over coffee! I nodded, laughed and teared up a few times as I read, remembering my early years of teaching music. I love how Jessica gives practical steps for success that will work with any teaching situation, but also encourages teachers to be their own unique person. Jessica reminds teachers that we are the exact music teacher our students need and we are there on purpose! Reading this book helped renew my passion for teaching elementary music as I enter my ninth year!"

Rachel Hammon

JESSICA PERESTA

"Jessica has been a huge help in getting me through the early years of teaching, and this book does not fall short of the compassion she has shown music teachers in other capacities. I found myself nodding and agreeing with every word I read, with a few "yes" and "amen" exclamations thrown in! I can't wait for other music teachers to get their hands on this book, and I look forward to gifting a copy to any emerging young educators I meet in the future."

Katie Holbrook

MAKE A NOTE

FOR GRANT, MY HUSBAND AND BIGGEST SUPPORTER.

YOU HAVE HELPED ME AND ENCOURAGED ME TO
FOLLOW MY DREAMS. I'M SO GRATEFUL FOR YOUR
LOVE AND FOR THE COUNTLESS HOURS YOU'VE SPENT
HELPING ME IN MY BUSINESS ENDEAVORS.

INTRO

In college, I completed every credit needed to earn my Bachelor of Music Education. After finishing my student teaching placement, I THOUGHT I felt prepared for teaching music in a school setting. Upon graduating in December, I fully planned to get a substitute teaching position until I could get a teaching job that following fall. Well, lo and behold, one music teaching position was available but there hadn't been a music program there for 7 years. Yes... 7 full years.

I quickly realized there were several things my instructors and mentors hadn't told me about teaching in my own classroom. Nobody told me that some days instead of teaching music, I would be dealing with behavior issues all day long. They didn't tell me I would almost daily feel like I was going to pee my pants from not being able to go to the bathroom. I definitely wasn't prepared for the attitudes and odors (and bodily fluids like pee that would end up on my floor) coming into my door each day.

Going from a student teaching placement to being the one and only teacher in my new classroom were two totally different things. To say I felt overwhelmed was an understatement. Have you heard the expression "fish out of water?" Well, I felt more like a whale out of the ocean. It was like... here's your comfortable life and you're going to trade it for a life of crying, doubting yourself, and nervousness all balled up with "But I also love these students of mine so dang much."

When you're a music teacher, a lot of times you feel like you're on an island all on your own. You're not quite sure where to turn to ask all the questions you have, so you just kind of slowly figure things out for yourself. But, you also turn to Google and type in things like "how to teach elementary music" and hope an answer, ANY helpful answer, will pop up on your screen.

If you're feeling overwhelmed, you're not alone. The training you receive in college teaches you the mechanics of what you really need to know when becoming an elementary music teacher. You learn all about teaching philosophies and how to teach students, but you really don't quite figure it out until you're thrown into your classroom and expected to just do it. All of a sudden, you're viewed as the expert and you quickly realize you're the one responsible for planning lessons and teaching music to multiple classes. Tag... you're it. Even if you're not ready, this is your classroom.

Through the process of reading the pages in this book, my hope is that you'll realize you're not alone in the way you might be feeling. Being a music teacher, although so very rewarding, is also extremely hard. There are so many things you aren't quite prepared for, and you may want to ask other music teachers if they're thinking, experiencing, or feeling the same way you are, but don't want to feel judged.

Well, I'm here to tell you that I get you. The other music teachers reading this book get you. You have a group of elementary music teachers all over the world who love you, support you, and can relate to exactly what you're going through. In this book, my goal is for you to truly realize that. From reading these pages, I hope you're able to feel a bit more confident in this role you've taken on as a music teacher. You're amazing and this calling has been set in front of you for a reason. So, take a deep breath and know that you can do this. You've been assigned to your classroom and to your students for a reason.

When you feel burnt out or overwhelmed, go back to your "why" you became a music teacher in the first place. Then, come back to this book as much as you need to so you can remind yourself that you can do this! Make note of all you've accomplished already and what you plan to accomplish moving forward in the future with your students. Make notes while you're reading, and then continue making beautiful notes with your students in music.

Chapter 1: What you need to know about life

The exhaustion you feel is normal

I'll never forget coming home after my first day of teaching and the sheer and utter exhaustion I felt. Honestly, there's really nothing to compare it to. I'm a mom to three little boys, and I'll still say there is definitely "no tired like teacher tired." During that first week of teaching, I remember coming home and just passing out on the couch. Then, I knew I needed to somehow muster up the energy to do it all over again the next day.

So, let's go back to "there's no tired like teacher tired." Let's change it to, "there's DEFINITELY no tired like music teacher tired." Don't get me wrong...all teachers are tired. Every...single...one of them. But, since I'm talking to my music teacher friends here, let's talk about why you're so tired, shall we?

You experienced tiredness in college (or so you thought.) But, you could take breaks between classes, and let's be honest, take a good nap if needed. Once you begin teaching, you end up shoving lunch down your throat in ten minutes flat most days. Going to the bathroom ends up feeling like a race against time. Also, let's talk about your plan time. Yes, you really need it to plan and will end up missing it some days due to assemblies (more on that later).

For an elementary music teacher, it's not just the normal walking up and down the hallways and standing up to teach. Oh no, my friend. You dance with your students, lift heavy instruments and risers, and sing AND talk all day long. Not to mention you give your all for your students and are completely using every ounce of energy to teach them every day. You also plan programs, work on lesson plans, attend professional development workshops, direct extracurricular honors choirs or Orff ensembles, deal with classroom management and behavior issues, and so much more.

On top of that, a lot of music teachers teach at more than one school, teach all of K-12 music if you're at a smaller school, have a side job like teaching private lessons or accompanying, and are also juggling everything at home. Your home life could include your spouse, kids, friends, house maintenance, groceries, laundry, etc. It's a never-ending hamster wheel you feel like you can't get off of and it's normal to feel exhausted. I mean, think about all you do throughout your day!

Eventually, you fall into a routine and get used to the tired feeling. After the first month of school, you realize you CAN make it and somehow manage to muster up enough energy to get through the day. It's so hard to take care of yourself though, but it's so important.

Here are some of my favorite self-care strategies:

- Exercise or go for a walk
- Do something you love once a week
- Try to leave school on time at least 3 days a week

- Go into school early to get things done so you CAN leave school on time
- Listen to your favorite podcast or music in your car
- Write down your thoughts. Putting what you're feeling on paper really helps relieve stress.
- Talk about how you feel with others you trust
- Get everything you need ready for the morning the night before
- Try to get enough sleep
- Meal plan and have simple dinners ready to go
- Have a plan for classroom management and stick to it
- Lesson plan and be prepared
- Give yourself the weekends to actually rest and relax (as much as you can)

As you can see, most of the things on this list are about taking care of yourself. I'll be the first to say that this is most definitely easier said than done. You're constantly taking care of others, so a lot of times taking care of you comes in last place. But, it's so important. Even if you just choose one of the things listed to begin implementing this week, you'll begin to feel better and ready to tackle the week ahead.

As for the teaching duties on the list, the more prepared you are the better. Stick with the plan you have in place for classroom management. Don't give up too soon. This is something that will cause a lot of exhaustion on your part. You constantly deal with talkers, wigglers, attitudes, and back-talking, and you just want to teach music. But, the more you stick with your classroom management plan and don't give up too soon on it (which we'll discuss more in detail later on in the book), then you'll be able to teach music more.

Teaching is a rewarding career, but it's also exhausting. You're not just physically pouring into your students every day, but also mentally and emotionally forming connections with them too. Please remember to give yourself lots of grace. You can't pour from an empty cup. Take care of yourself, so you can in turn take care of others. Listen to your body and what it needs. If you feel extra tired on a certain day, try to go to bed early. Give yourself breaks, even throughout the school day, to take a quick sip of water or sit down for 10 seconds between classes.

It just takes time to get into a routine as a music teacher. It really is so fast-paced and go, go, go all the time. You feel like you're constantly needing to stay "on" and need to keep your energy up for your students. It's such a joy to teach music, and an honor that you get to be the one to pour into the lives of these kiddos day in and day out, but it's also okay to realize that it's exhausting at the same time.

This exhaustion you feel isn't just because you're tired. It's so much more than that. At the end of each week, you feel ready for the weekend because you've shown up in an act of service and love all week long.

You'll get sick a lot

"I became a music teacher so I could get sick all the time," said no teacher ever. But, this is just something that comes right along with the job. You think your immune system can handle all the germ-infested kids you come into contact with each and every day, but your body has just never experienced anything like this before. Drink plenty of water, wash your hands a lot, and have hand sanitizer at the ready all day every day.

Although these things help a little bit, you notice you still wake up after week one feeling sicker than you've been since you were a kid. So, what should you do? Call in sick! Yes. Seriously. Your sick days are yours. There's so much guilt that goes into taking a sick day for yourself. But, please know that the sick days given to you are there for a reason. When you show up to school sick, you'll just get sicker and possibly pass it on to others. You are a much more effective teacher when you show up to school healthy and ready to teach. After your first year of teaching, it's almost like you develop a protective shield that protects you against germs. You still get sick, but it's definitely nothing like what you experience during your year one.

"But, I can't get a sub", you've probably already said out loud. Do you know what I say to that? You may not get a sub. But, it's alright to put yourself first. If you've done your part by having the sub plans ready and have called in for a sub, then you've done your part. As much as it's not ideal for your school to pull in a member of the support staff or to combine your classes with the art classes for the day, unfortunately sometimes this is just part of the deal.

Work-life balance isn't real

When you get your first teaching position, you don't realize how much of a human juggler you'll become. I'm not talking about the kind of juggler who can keep 3 balls in the air for an extended period of time. But, on a side note, if you can do that, I'm seriously so impressed. I'm talking about the kind of juggling where you feel pulled in multiple directions at once and aren't sure which task to accomplish first or last.

If you're a parent you've got that ball to juggle, then you've got the other family and friends ball, along with the taking care of home tasks ball, and also any side jobs like teaching private lessons or tutoring ball. That's a lot of juggling you do each and every day as an elementary music teacher. This is something you maybe didn't realize would be so tough when you decided to pursue this career path. But, although it's tough, it is possible to maintain a healthy balance in every area of your life.

I want you to consider that work-life balance will look different for everyone, because it is, after all, your life. Your life and personality (which we'll talk more about in a minute) don't look like anyone else's. That's good news though because that means there's only one you!

For me, when I started my teaching career, I was single and living with 4 other roommates. Then, I met my now-husband 2 months later. We got married, then had our first son 3 years later, and then I became a working mom. Now, I have 3 sons and am still married. So, as you see, since starting my first teaching job to now, my home life has changed over the years.

My work life after college started with me teaching elementary music full time, accompanying two children choirs, and teaching several piano students. Holy wow that makes me tired just reading that. I then continued teaching full time at school, and then when I got married and had my first child, I stopped accompanying and just taught a few piano students. Now, I run my music education business but am juggling mom life at the same time.

What does your life look like right now? Are you struggling to find a work-life balance you so desperately want? No matter how your life looks, learning to thrive in life, not just survive is so important. Let go of any of the guilt you're feeling about not pouring more time into an area of your life and just focus on doing the best you can. That will help relieve so much of the pressure you've put on yourself.

Let's talk about the word balance. I actually HATE the word balance. I used to think that every day had to look the same. I tried to make sure every hour of my day was equally devoted to work and to home life and that stressed me out so much. Then, I shifted my thinking to realize that balance will look different each day and that's okay! Some days, I pour so much into my home and personal life and some days work needs more of my focus. But, at the end of the week, the balance is there. It honestly all equals out in the end, even when the hours aren't divided up perfectly.

Let's dive more into the strategies that have worked for me, and so many other music teachers I've worked with, that will help you as you begin to implement them. Don't feel overwhelmed looking at this list, but choose just one to start with this week.

1. Prioritize your tasks

You have so many tasks on your to-do list every day. It's so hard to know how to prioritize your tasks to not feel overly stressed out every day. "Prioritize" means to determine the order for dealing with (a series of items or tasks) according to their relative importance. When you think about that, what are the top priorities in your life? How can you make sure they are at the top of your list and not stuck somewhere at the bottom?

Like I said earlier, your life doesn't look like anyone else's, so your priorities will all look a little different as well. Also, let's remember what I just mentioned about balance. Prioritizing your tasks doesn't mean making everything balanced perfectly. No, not at all.

I'm a huge list maker. I always have been, and I have a list for everything. Paper lists, Google docs, Google calendar, the notes app on my phone, voice memos. You name it and I've probably done it. Making lists helps me keep my life in order. When I put on my calendar what's happening each month, I can make a list of what needs to get done each day, week, or month. This helps me to not just fly by the seat of my pants, and to actually be able to prioritize what needs to get done when.

Put the big tasks on your calendar first. These are things like doctor's appointments, school programs, or your child's weekly piano lessons, for example. Then, fill in the "other" things on your calendar. This is when you'll put in things like "go grocery shopping", "work on lesson plans", or even "clean the house." You're basically just penciling in what needs to get done around what you already have on your calendar. After putting the things on your calendar, you can visually see and prioritize what needs to get done. You can also plan when you want or need to complete these tasks and won't feel like your brain is spinning.

2. Work efficiently

What do I mean by work efficiently? You already show up every day and give your all, so working even harder isn't possible. But, I'm not talking about working harder, but smarter.

What does this mean exactly? Well, one of my favorite ways to work more efficiently is to start work early. I'll be the first to admit that I went from struggling to get up when my alarm went off every day to loving the mornings. This is the time of day I can get more done, where I feel like my mind is truly able to focus on the task at hand, and I feel like I can cross the most off of my to-do list.

When you get a lot done in the morning, even just 30 minutes before your contract time starts, there's less you need to tackle during your planning period or after school. After school, you'll need to stay late some days. But, you're also going to be tired from a full day of teaching and are ready to leave for the day. There will be days you need to stay late to finish up planning for a program, work on lesson plans, or set up for the next day, but try to leave on time when you can.

Another way to work more efficiently is to knock off tasks on your to-do list during your plan time. Remember to prioritize your task, so during your planning period (if you have one), you'll know exactly what to begin working on first, second, third, and so on. What days of the week are important to get things done? When are your lesson plans due? Do you need to enter grades by a certain date? When you have a list made, with tasks numbered from the most to least important, you'll get so much more done.

The last tip for working more efficiently is to write down everything so you know when there are upcoming meetings, assemblies, or field trips. Then, look at what you've planned to teach, and adjust your plans accordingly. Make notes next to which class missed a certain lesson or if you didn't quite finish a full lesson plan sequence. Knowing ahead of time about what's coming will help you keep track of things.

3. It's okay to say "no"

You're pushed and pulled in so many different directions. It feels like there are so many people in your life needing things, and sometimes all at once. It can be a little overwhelming trying to please everyone.

I'm the biggest people pleaser there is. For years, I had a case of the "I don't want to hurt anyone's feelings", so I end up saying yes to everything and everyone. It was exhausting to live like that. Then, I began to really learn how to say no. It was so freeing and really caused my anxiety to go away because I realized the importance of taking care of me too.

If a teacher needed me to teach her class a certain song, but I knew I had no extra time on my plate, I said no. Sometimes I would say "not right now" or "I can later", but the instant yes dissipated. When a family member wanted me to come over for dinner, but I was exhausted, I said "let's choose another night." If my husband (once I got married) wanted to watch a movie on a school night, but I knew I wanted to go to bed early, I'd say something like, "let's watch that this weekend instead."

You see, the art of saying no takes time. This isn't something that comes naturally to us people-pleasers, but with time, you'll notice it gets easier and easier to do. Then, you won't feel like at the end of the week you're so mentally exhausted trying to meet these unrealistic expectations that have been put on you by others. The other people in your life don't know your schedule and life as you do. So, when they ask you to do something, they may not realize you truly just don't have time. Saying no isn't a hurtful response, but a way of saying "I'm ok putting my needs first."

4. Self-care isn't selfish

Self-care isn't selfish, and the quicker you realize this, the less overwhelmed you'll begin to feel. We talked earlier about not being a constant people pleaser. Acknowledge the fact that you need to take care of yourself too, and then actually do it!

Everyone has a different personality. You might be an introvert, extrovert, or a combination of both of them. The first step is to acknowledge your personality and what your needs are. Know your personality type, when you've reached your limit, and when you need a break.

How do you take care of yourself? Well, this depends on you! You're a unique individual with things you enjoy doing and ways you like to unwind that won't look like anyone else. There are so many ways self-care can happen for you, and the main goal is to just take care of yourself. Go for that walk, watch your favorite show, or even go for a drive to clear your head. Include space in your calendar for fun with friends, things you like to do, mini getaways, or even day trips.

Not only that, make time to really unplug and know that those texts, emails, or even social media posts can wait. Of course, you'll want to stay in the loop with what's happening in your family and friends' lives, but if you don't get back right away, that's okay! You're allowed to put yourself first sometimes. On top of that, don't feel guilty about not being able to spend as much time with friends during the busy seasons. Taking care of yourself is necessary to be in the best mental shape to take care of others. You can't pour from an empty cup, and you'll soon find yourself feeling depleted when you come last.

One day you'll have a family

One of the good things about getting married and having a baby after I started teaching, was the fact that I already had a well-established routine down. I was way more comfortable in my own skin, then I was as a first-year teacher. The transition wasn't hard as a teacher, but it was in becoming a parent. Now, I had to get me and a child ready for the day, get up way earlier than I was used to, and I wanted to leave school on time so I could spend some time with my son.

If you're reading this book and you're not a parent, that's definitely fine. Maybe reading this chapter will help you understand co-workers who have had kids and how life changed for them in the process. But, if you're reading this and you're a parent, I want you to kick that guilt you might be feeling to the curb. If you're a working parent, sometimes you have days where you have to bring work home. There are also days you need to go in earlier or stay later for whatever reason. You're always going to feel a push and pull between your work and home life. It's so hard, but you need to know that every parent feels this way at one point or another.

Realize that your family comes first though. Work is important and I fully believe you can be passionate about both your work and home life. But, you also need to set boundaries on your time as well. Don't feel guilty about taking personal days and about taking sick days for you or your child.

If you're feeling worn out or like you need more help, lean on your resources. You may have family and friends, or even co-workers willing to help you out when needed. Sometimes, all you need to do is ask. If you need a date night, help watching your child during a program, a babysitter during the day, or even someone to run an errand for you, state what you need. Once I learned to share responsibilities and admit that I really couldn't do it all, it helped me out so much.

The other thing I want to mention about having a family is to find life hacks to simplify things. Think about things like grocery pickup, drive-thru oil changes, online banking, and meal planning to have easy meals in the freezer or to throw in the crockpot. Other ways to make life simpler and your days run smoother are to layout yours and your child's clothes the night before, have lunches made and ready to go, and give yourself way more time than you think you'll need to get ready in the morning.

Others won't understand your job

You're so excited to be a music teacher and want to share about what goes on in your teaching life with your family and friends. You can tell after having a couple of conversations that they don't understand your job. No one will ever be as excited or passionate about teaching music to kids as you are! Although the people in your life support what you do and might even be excited to see you following your dreams and passions, they just don't get it. Many of them still think about elementary music as sitting and singing songs. They haven't received the years of teacher training, done research and planning, or been in your classroom teaching music day in and day out.

My husband is an IT specialist. There is so much more to his job title than that. But, do you want to know the funny thing? At the time of writing this book, we've been married for 14 years. Although he's worked different jobs in his field, I still don't understand his job. I support him in his career, but as he tries to explain to me what he does every day, it goes right over my head. This isn't because I'm not interested or am not paying attention to what he's saying. It's because the passion he has for his career and his work can only come from him.

You see, you have a passion for what you do for a reason. Not everyone is given the same calling in life, and that's a good thing! The world truly needs the different gifts that everyone brings to it. I can't imagine if we were all music teachers. That would be so boring! Of course so much beautiful music would still be made. But, I believe music teachers are who should be teaching music.

If you've had a conversation with a friend while out to dinner, and they seem like they're uninterested, they may not be. Keep in mind that they may not be aware of what you're talking about. They don't understand putting on performances, planning lessons, teaching different grade levels, different teaching methods, or all of the other things that go into teaching elementary music. They're not supposed to know, because you're the one who has the degree or certification to teach your students. Of course, still talk about what you do! Your family and friends will ask about it and will show genuine interest. Explain it in the simplest of terms so they can understand, while showing interest in what they do in their career as well.

Chapter 2: What you need to know about feelings

You're on an island all on your own

Most of the teachers at your school have other teachers to collaborate with when it comes to planning and discussing how to implement their lessons. For example, there's a 1st-grade team, 2nd-grade team, and so on. They get to bounce ideas off of each other, ask for feedback, and even split the students into various small groups for math and reading.

Your team usually consists of yourself, the art teacher, P.E. teacher, librarian, and computer teacher. This is a team that can relate to you in a lot of ways when it comes to being a "specials" or "enrichment" teacher. But, they can't relate to you as the music teacher. You can't go to them and ask how they begin teaching rhythm to their 2nd graders because you'll get a deer in the headlights look.

It's so easy to feel like you're on an island on your own some days. You have many questions about lesson planning, classroom management, implementing and teaching the lessons, and even about different teaching methodologies, but don't know where to go to ask those questions. If you're feeling overwhelmed and alone, please know that these feelings are normal. I can't tell you the number of music teachers I've met who say they've felt the exact same way as me. This is something that just isn't talked about enough. No one in college filled you in on the fact that you might feel a bit lonely as an elementary music teacher.

You assumed everyone would appreciate you and there would be someone, or just anyone, that you could talk about planning, teaching, and to collaborate with. This will come. I promise it gets easier. When you're having a down day, or feel lonely, go back to your why. Remember why you became a music teacher in the first place and that your purpose is to teach music to your students. As long as you're doing that, you'll be reminded each and every day by sweet smiles, hugs, and high fives, why you became a music teacher over everything else.

There is good news though. You can help yourself get off of that island by sharing and collaborating with other music teachers. Yes, these teachers are more than likely not at your school. So, you need to be creative in finding ways to connect with other teachers and forming relationships. It might just take a bit more work and patience.

Relationships take time and consistency

Another way to get off of that music teacher island is to work on forming relationships with the other teachers and staff at your school. You maybe feel like they don't appreciate you or value your job because you've heard other music teachers say this is just how it goes. You may have received a negative comment, so you just assume this is how everyone feels. This is just not true. I'm the biggest over-analyzer of all time. These exact situations happened to me and I would get quiet, become awkward, and not talk to other teachers.

I realized it wasn't just about forming relationships with my students that mattered, but also with my coworkers. When I started out, no one knew me. Everyone was cordial and kind, but just like in a new relationship, it takes time. What I would assume was other teachers not wanting to get to know me, was sometimes them just being busy. When they were in a rush to drop their classes off to music, it was because they had a lot of planning to get done. If they weren't wanting to chat with me in the teachers' lounge, it was sometimes due to them simply needing a moment of quiet.

You see, just as much as music teachers want to feel supported, the same can be said for the regular classroom teachers. There is a lot of misinformation out there about regular classroom teachers not respecting or appreciating the position of elementary music teachers. But that's not always the case. There's sometimes misunderstanding all around from everyone.

What can alleviate some of this? Forming relationships of course. Wrong assumptions are made when you just don't know the other teachers very well. So, how do you do this?

Some of my favorite ways are to:

- Be friendly
- Say hello in the hallway
- Talk to the teachers in the car rider line
- Make it a point to sit at different tables during staff meetings
- Attend Friday happy hour when you can
- Stay patient
- Remember that relationships take time
- Be true to who you are

No matter how you decide to form relationships with the other staff members in your building, do it with love and kindness. Remember that relationships take work, but with time you'll be amazed at some of the incredible relationships you're able to make. Some of the teachers who were the hardest to get to know will become your biggest advocates for the music program.

Find an online community

What can you do to help you "row, row, row your boat" right off of that island? Surround yourself with a community of music teachers who can relate to exactly what you're going through. The community you surround yourself with will come in many different forms. It takes a while to find music teachers you can relate to, but once you do, you'll begin to see instant growth happen. So, how do you connect with other music teachers online? There are several different ways.

First off, let's discuss Facebook groups. It's honestly a trial and error thing to find the right fit for you and your needs. I used to be in tons of teacher groups, but it got overwhelming trying to keep up with everything teachers were saying in them. So, I chose to stay in groups based on what I needed to help me grow as an educator. I also started my own Facebook groups, one for any elementary music teacher called "The Elementary Music Teacher Community" and another one for my HARMONY membership teachers.

Another great way to find online community is on Instagram. This has quickly become one of my favorite platforms and where I've connected with so many amazing music teachers. There are so many music teachers sharing ideas and collaborating with each other. This, like a Facebook group, is where you get the most out of it by what you put in. If you want to get supportive direct messages, be the first one to send an encouraging message. If you want comments on your posts, then be the first to comment on other posts. I have met so many amazing educators on Instagram who have been guests on my podcast, whom I've collaborated with in one way or another, and who have become personal friends of mine.

There's also an active Twitter community where teachers share ideas and even have scheduled dates where they use hashtags for a question and answer time. Basically, find what you're comfortable with and how you want to stay connected and do it. Don't overwhelm yourself trying to be on every social media channel, but find what works for you.

Find an in-person community

Of course, connecting online is so important. With the day and age we're living in, it's so amazing that through the click of a mouse, you can literally go anywhere you want to online. But, with that said, connecting with others in person is still vital and important.

My favorite ways to connect in person are through workshops, training, levels courses (think Orff or Kodaly), and conventions. At these events, you meet other music educators who may or may not work at a school near you. You learn so much from the other music teachers you come into contact with by just observing them, asking questions, and learning right along with them. Some of my best inspiration came from just one or two ideas presented at an in-person conference. There would also be a teacher who might say one sentence that ended up sticking with me and helping me reframe the way I do things in my classroom.

Don't forget the value of staying connected with the other music education students you went to college with is (if you got your music education certificate this way). Even though you'll probably be spread out all over the map, staying in contact with them is so important. Try to meet up in person from time to time to share ideas and talk about your struggles and wins you're having in your classroom.

Music teachers are qualified professionals too

I can't tell you the number of times I was asked if I needed a degree to teach music. People honestly don't understand what goes on in an elementary music classroom. Back in my elementary school days, the music class looked way different than it does now. Others who aren't aware of what goes on in the music classroom may feel that any person from the street could come into the music room to sing songs all day long. You and I know there is much more that goes into teaching music than that.

It's so easy as music teachers to feel like what you do day in and day out goes unnoticed. You want someone, ANYONE for that matter, to acknowledge that what you're doing matters. That's why others thinking of you as an unqualified professional bothers music teachers so much.

But, I want to tell you this. For every negative comment that comes your way or person who makes you feel like your job doesn't matter, there will be someone right behind them cheering you on. You'll have so many supportive teachers and parents who want the music program to succeed. Also, don't forget about that community of other music educators who are there to support you along the way too. Go into work every day with your head held high, knowing that you get to teach music to kids every single day. Because of you, lives are being changed and kids are learning in ways they never knew were possible.

JESSICA PERESTA

Some students won't like music class

I'll never forget my first year teaching music. Not only was I at a school that didn't have music for seven years, but I also started in the middle of the school year. My new students stared blankly at me as I tried singing and doing body percussion activities with them. They acted like I was trying to teach them a foreign language (which I of course did with multi-cultural songs later on). Music was new to these kids and they just didn't understand what I was trying to do.

Over the years, most of my students loved coming to music class. I developed relationships with these kids, and in fact some of them I still speak with today. Although a lot of them enjoyed learning music, there were those few where no matter what I did, they just weren't having it. I could have sang their very favorite song in the universe, and they would still give me eye rolls or body language that showed me they just didn't want to be there. It completely hurt my feelings, and of course, I took it personally.

Weren't these kids supposed to enjoy music class? What was I doing wrong? Didn't they realize how lucky they were to have me since there hadn't been music at their school for so long? Do I need to just get through this semester and start fresh in the fall?

I then remembered that with anything else in life, it just takes time. As music educators, we show up for every student, whether it feels like they've shown up for us or not too. Sometimes you'll see these "hard to teach" kids come around and begin enjoying music, then sometimes they'll leave your school and you'll wonder if you made even the slightest impact at all.

So, how can you encourage these students to still want to come to music class? How can you make sure you're not feeling overwhelmed and frustrated every day you get a certain class walking through your doors?

There are some children who are not as talented in singing, playing instruments, or keeping a steady beat as other children. If you see a child struggling, just giving them a simple phrase like "you're doing a great job", "I have seen so much improvement in you" or even "look how well you are keeping a steady beat" can go such a long way. The child will feel like they are getting the hang of it, and will want to keep improving. Over time, you will see musical growth in that child. Encouragement truly does go a long way. Even if you don't see growth right away, sometimes these are the kids who will come back to see you when they're in middle or high school and thank you for making an impact in their life. This happened to me several times and my jaw almost hit the floor.

Keep striving to form a relationship with these kids. It will seem like with certain students you'll need to work a lot harder at connecting and forming a relationship with them. But, don't give up. Sometimes kids who aren't participating or have said the dreaded words, "I hate music class" don't really mean it. There are underlying things there that you may not know about. Also, these kids probably give a lackluster effort in a lot of their classes and not just yours.

If you get pushback from your students, and you can tell what you're teaching isn't resonating with them, then change it up. Truly know your students and teach music that is relevant to them. Really make it a point to teach music that reaches them and not just what you THINK they should learn. It's ok not to just regurgitate something you learned at a workshop and to make a lesson your own. Once you do this, you'll notice a shift in some of your students' behaviors who are giving you the biggest pushback. All of a sudden, they'll realize how much you care because you're making an effort to really create lessons that make them engage in music.

There are many opinions thrown your way

Maybe you haven't taught at a school where you've started a music program from scratch, but you may have followed in another music teacher's footsteps. Students are expecting you to do things like their former music teacher. The teachers and parents probably have certain ideas of how they "think" the music program should be run. It can feel like nothing you do is quite good enough because you're not Mr. or Ms. previous teacher. With so many opinions coming your way, things can start to feel overwhelming. You'll be caught in the trap of wanting to please everyone, and may start to lose your teaching philosophy a bit in the process.

As the music teacher, think of you interacting with the administrators, teachers, parents, and students as a dating relationship. They accept the fact that you're the music teacher and you must have a little bit of an idea of what you're doing, even if you feel like an imposter some days. Each day, week, month, and year that you show up to teach music, those opinions start to dwindle and you're able to do things the way you want to. Relationships are slowly starting to form and trust is being built.

As you keep teaching year after year, when opinions are thrown your way, you'll be able to listen and discern what is being suggested. Sometimes the ideas will be useful, and you'll think "why didn't I think of that." Then other times the opinions make absolutely no sense. Just like when responding to others when you're asked if you need a degree to teach music, just answer in kindness when opinions are given to you. You can always say something like, "thank you so much for that suggestion" and then move on. If it makes you feel better, even the general classroom teachers are given constant opinions from their parents.

It's alright to cry

I wish I could count on my fingers the number of times I left school crying. There were certain days, or even weeks, that things just plain sucked. It felt like I was dealing with so many things besides just teaching (which we'll discuss more in chapter 4) and it was hard. I would cry leaving school over several different things. Sometimes it was because of what was going on in the personal lives of some of my students. Other times it was because a lesson plan bombed. Then, there were times I just felt frustrated for various things that had gone on during the day.

A teacher who tells you they've never cried over a botched lesson, a hard day, or an exhausting week, isn't telling you the truth. I know teachers who have taught for 25 years who still have hard days. Crying is actually a good thing. Sometimes a good cry is all you need to release those emotions you've held onto all day.

There are days you don't feel like going to school for one reason or another. Maybe you're dealing with something hard in your personal life. Maybe last week was hard, so the thought of going back for a new week is the last thing you want to do. Maybe teaching music is way harder than you thought it would be, and you're just ready to wave the white flag. I've dealt with every single one of these situations, and I've cried many times about these things as well. Here's the kicker... I'm not a crier. Yes, I'm serious. I've never been a very emotional person, but I've cried several times over being a music teacher.

On the flip side of things, you've also cried about positive things. The first time you see that lightbulb moment in a student you've been hoping to reach will make you cry. When a performance you've been working so hard on for months on end comes together, it will make you cry. When 70+ students are singing in unison at once from the stage, you'll definitely tear up. There are so many hard things that make you cry in your car, but there are also so many positive things that bring you tears of joy as well.

There are days you want to give up

There may be days you want to just throw in the towel. There are moments where you wonder if this is really what you signed up for. It seems much harder than you thought it would be when you decided to become a music teacher.

Please realize these thoughts and emotions are completely normal. Think about any other job you've had before. Did you like every single second of every day you were there? I mean, maybe. But for me, I've been a camp counselor, worked as a carhop at Sonic, worked at Dillard's, and worked in the library on my college campus. I've also had several piano accompanist jobs, taught private piano lessons, and of course, taught elementary music. There were good and bad days in each of these jobs.

Some days you don't want to teach music because of the way the kids are treating you. Some days you just wake up with a case of the "I don't wannas". Some days are just so hard, that you don't know if you can do it anymore.

Just like I can guarantee you'll continue to have hard days, I also know there will keep being amazing days too. Stick it out on those tough days. The good truly does outweigh the bad, and you'll keep finding those moments of joy we talked about earlier. Remember that you became a music teacher for a reason. You could have been anything else in the whole world, but you became a music teacher. On the days you feel like throwing up the peace sign and walking out, think about your why.

Feel those feelings

I've already talked about it being ok to cry, but what about the other gamut of emotions you feel from time to time. You're not a robot but are a human being. Feeling emotions is not only normal but important. There are hard days, good days, sad days, happy days, and everything in between.

In order to break down that imaginary wall between you and your students, show your human side from time to time. No, I'm not meaning to just stand in front of them and be a blubbering mess while crying hysterically. But if you do that, that's okay! I've shown kids my emotions. Then, when doing that, they feel permission to show theirs. They see you as human and relatable and feel comfortable talking to you about the hard things that might be going on with them.

Unexpected things happen in life and outside the school walls. There might be a sudden death in the family, or you may go into labor while leaving school (speaking from experience here), or there may be a tragedy in your city or school. There are days that are difficult to show up to school to teach because something hard happened the night before or that morning. This might be something like knowing your child is sick, and a Grandparent is staying home with them so you can work. Then, you kind of feel like you're just going through the motions that day because your heart is somewhere else. Feel those feelings. Let yourself be human. Go into the bathroom between classes on "those" days and pray, take a moment of silence, or get your thoughts together.

Chapter 3: What you need to know about the first year

Your first year is really hard

I imagine if you're reading this chapter you're either about to enter your first year of teaching, you're somewhere in the middle of it, or you're wrapping up the first year. Whatever category you find yourself in, I want you to realize something. Your first year really is that hard. If you think you're the only one struggling while trying to figure out "all the things", you most definitely are not.

Gone are the days where you're a student teacher and your cooperating teacher is there to give you advice. You'll realize that quickly the first time a class walks into your music room. You look around the room and all of these little eyeballs are staring back at you waiting for you to teach them music. Imposter syndrome almost immediately kicks in, and your heart starts beating a million miles a minute. Then, you just jump in and start teaching because this is what you prepared for.

But... you then find out that all of these grand ideas and lessons you had planned out end up not going so well. Some of the lessons are a total flop in fact. In your head, you thought you would show up and teach music, and every child would immediately be grateful and excited. This is not how things go down at all.

Not all days are bad or hard. But, you second guess almost every decision you make. You're constantly being stretched and pulled in many different directions. You want to figure it all out right away, but quickly realize things just take time. In fact, you started teaching because you wanted to teach music, but are finding that there is so much more in being a music teacher than you ever realized.

If you're entering your first year of teaching in elementary music from a secondary position, are returning to teaching after taking a few years off, or if you've moved to a new school, it can feel like your first year all over again too. Those first year teacher feelings, thoughts, and emotions will definitely come to the surface again.

Why is the first year so hard? Well, there are a few reasons. There is so much more to teaching elementary music than just teaching. You'll quickly find you're now a parent figure, counselor, nurse, custodian, secretary, and babysitter all in one day. Right along with teaching, you'll also find out that you need to make copies, set up for classes coming in, spend lots of time planning, get programs prepared, reply to emails, attend professional development, and assess your students. No, it's definitely not just about teaching music at all.

Just like you're figuring out how to do "all the things", your students are figuring you out. You'll notice that during your first year of teaching, when you're unconfident and unsure about teaching, your students won't respond as well as you'd hope they would. Also, students need to get used to you, your procedures, the classroom management you have in place, your teaching style, and music class in general in some cases.

Remember to give yourself grace and remind yourself that you're learning what to do and not to do during your first year. It's a learning curve and a lot of it is done by trial and error. Just put one foot in front of the other while continuing to move forward. You will make mistakes and are going to mess up. But, all of this is completely normal and you will get through it just like so many teachers before you have. These mistakes are what will cause you to grow the most as a teacher.

What to do before you step foot into your classroom

You're so excited to step into your classroom and teach for the first time. But, there are a few things that need to happen before you do. Doing the things mentioned in this section ahead of time will help you set yourself up for success as you begin your first year.

First, you'll need to set up your classroom. When I set up my classroom for the first time, it was just kind of a guessing game of what to put where. I was like, "I guess I'll put chairs here and a drum over here. Yeah, that looks good." But, there was no rhyme or reason behind it. I don't know about you, but for me, my classroom management class in college was geared towards regular classroom teachers. Also, the teaching Praxis test only asked questions about arranging the classroom with desks for a general classroom setting. I had observed several music classes during practicums and my student teaching experience, but still didn't really understand why teachers arranged their rooms the way they did. I should have asked more questions but thought I would just be able to figure it out on my own.

The next thing you'll want to do before seeing students is get all the "stuff" in order. The stuff includes class lists, lesson planning templates, assessment sheets, classroom decorations, procedures you're going to post, any copies you'll need to make before the first week, and making sure all technology is ready to go. You'll also want to have your teaching resources organized and easily accessible. Don't worry if you don't have the planning process down yet. This comes with time and you'll figure out a routine and the way you want to do things. But, have as much stuff ready to go beforehand so you're not trying to do all the things the first week of school and can focus on teaching your students.

It's okay to be you and not like the teacher down the street

One of the things that's so easy to do as elementary music teachers is to compare yourself to every other teacher. You think you have a good plan in place, have your philosophy of teaching ready to go, and are so excited to dive right in with your students. But, once you begin going to workshops, see or hear the way other teachers do things with their students, and get to look at other classrooms, you start feeling a bit insecure. Maybe you've always been a pretty confident person, but all of a sudden you feel like you're not doing a good enough job.

How do I know this? Because this is exactly what happened to me. Yes, I started in the middle of the school year. Yes, I had no teaching resources and had to figure things out all on my own. But, I still walked into my classroom with confidence and ready to teach music to my new set of students. But then, I attended my first Saturday workshop at another school. I walked into this music room and saw all the drums, rhythm instruments, teaching manipulatives, mallet instruments, and student computers, and my jaw almost hit the floor. I noticed it all and I became insecure.

I remember returning back to my classroom that following Monday with thoughts like, "who are you to teach music", or "your students would get a much better experience with that music teacher who has been teaching for years", or even, "you don't even have any instruments, so you can't do any music with these kids." Yes, I thought all of that and so much more. All of a sudden I went from confident to insecure.

It's so easy to compare yourself to other music teachers in person or online. But, here's something exciting I want you to hear. You get to be completely you in your classroom! Isn't that a freeing thought? There's only one you and I truly believe your students need the exact teacher and person that you are. You have a unique personality and things you're good at. There are also qualities that set you apart and a musical background that you get to bring to your students.

Want to know what else? You also get to choose how you want to teach music. Explore the different teaching methods to find out what you can relate to most. Go to Orff or Kodaly workshops, attend a levels course, ask other music teachers how they developed their teaching style, and then slowly figure out yours. It takes time to find what works for you. But, you also can combine approaches (which is completely my style), and change things up as you go too. I like pulling from multiple teaching methods and approaches. It took me time to figure this out though. Then, I became much more confident as an educator once I remembered why I became a music teacher in the first place. I identified my unique qualities, and found my teaching style.

Don't compare your beginning to someone else's middle or end of their teaching career. You honestly don't know how they started out. During their first year of teaching, they may have found themselves facing the same overwhelm and falling into the comparison trap the same way you are. Keep putting one foot in front of the other, make a plan for how you want to teach, write down what instruments and resources you'd like to purchase each year, then keep moving forward.

Your mentor teacher may not know much about music

You get your first job and you're assigned a mentor teacher. You're so excited to pick this teacher's brain during your first year of teaching. You assume this teacher will know so much about music and will be ready and available to answer any questions you have throughout the school year. But, this isn't always the case.

This was definitely my plan. I was so excited to meet my mentor teacher. She was a 3rd-grade teacher at my school. Although she had been a previous drama teacher, she didn't know anything about music. Also, since I was new and I started in the middle of the school year, I didn't have many connections with other music teachers in my district. I knew my elementary music cooperating teacher and my college music professors, but that was about it.

My mentor teacher was busy planning her own lessons, teaching her class, communicating with parents, and needing to go to department meetings. Although she was helpful, there would sometimes be a delay in getting a question answered. So, I would spend a lot of time just figuring out things on my own as I went along.

But, I have fully learned that just getting in there and doing the hard things is the way I learn the best. Trust yourself and that you have what it takes to teach music effectively. Remember that you were hired for your position at your school for a reason. You may not have all the answers right now, but you'll get there. You'll never stop learning and are going to keep constantly growing as a teacher each and every year.

On top of having your mentor teacher, there are several other ways you can get mentorship. I already mentioned reaching out to your cooperating teacher and previous college professors. The former cooperating teacher might have another student teacher they're mentoring, so helping you might be hard. They'll have good intentions but are pressed for time. But, don't hesitate to reach out with questions if you need to. Don't get your feelings hurt if they take a while to get back to you though. This happened to me a few times. I'd have one of my former student teachers reach out to me as they were a first-year teacher, while I was also mentoring a student teacher. I've always had a heart for helping other music teachers and would respond the best I could, but there would sometimes be a delay in me answering them.

Another way to get mentorship is at workshops and professional development opportunities. Of course, right off the bat, you won't have these connections available to you. Just know that eventually, you'll meet so many other music teachers who you will be able to learn so much from. Connect with others from your district, surrounding districts, in your state, or in other states. Look for teachers who have similar teaching styles and completely different teaching styles, because you will learn from each of them. These experiences will stretch you and help you grow as a teacher more than any formal mentorship opportunity could. It also, of course, depends on your personality and learning style. For me, seeing what other music teachers were doing, asking questions, and being able to take notes allowed me to apply things easily to my classroom.

You can also get mentorship online. When I started out in my teaching career, social media wasn't a thing. Facebook came out during my first year of teaching. Whoa, that's crazy even to type. So, honestly, all I had were in-person connections, email capability, and the phone. It's so awesome now how much mentorship happens online. Look back at chapter 2 to review the different ways to find those connections with other teachers online.

The best mentor though is the teacher down the hallway. You're going to have so many questions you need to be answered in real-time. Find those teachers at your school that you connect with. Yes, they won't be music teachers (unless you work at a school that has multiple elementary music teachers), but they'll still be able to help you out. Maybe you connect well with the art teacher Or maybe there's a second-grade teacher who you feel comfortable talking to. I promise the other teachers at your school want the best for you. They've all been first teachers before, so they get it. No one wants to see you fail, they want their students to learn music, and you'll find that support system you need. Just don't be afraid to ask and have the conversations you need to help you grow.

You'll spend lots of your own money

I found out pretty fast that not every music teacher will have a budget to spend. After walking into my classroom in the middle of the school year with no resources or instruments, I knew I needed to get "all the things." After asking about having school money to spend, I found out I would be allotted one hundred dollars. I'm pretty sure my jaw went all the way to the floor. I was not expecting to hear that low of an amount at all. There are ways of course to get funding for what you need for your classroom. There's DonorsChoose, grants, PTA funds, district stipends, and your school budget. But, going into your first year, you're more than likely going to need to spend some of your money upfront.

A lot of it depends on the school you find yourself working at as well. Are you following in the footsteps of a teacher who left you a ton of resources you can use? Did your cooperating teacher or another teacher (maybe one who's retiring or has resources they're wanting to part ways with) give you some things for your classroom? Does your school you were hired at already have a nice budget set aside for the music department? Or, are you walking into a school without a lot of funding and you're basically given a smile and a "good luck" as you head into your classroom for the first time like I did?

As a first-year teacher, knowing your teaching situation, making a list of what you need after taking inventory in your new classroom, and then determining what funds (if any) you'll have available to you is so helpful. Go in with a plan of action and set money aside if you need to. But, also remember that each year you'll be able to purchase more, will have time to plan it out better, and will have more ways to apply for the money you're needing. Don't compare yourself to other teachers around you who have so much. I promise you, most of them started out exactly where you're at right now. They thought the same thoughts, experienced the same emotions, and wondered where in the world the necessary money will come from to provide music education to their students.

It's ok to start with nothing. This was my story, remember? Don't let the fact that you might have so little hold you back from teaching your students music. They don't know if the school down the street has 84 djembes and xylophones and you only have one total instrument. Also, your students don't know if you can't afford to buy things you need with your own money. Just do what you can, and trust that the rest will come with time. Then, work with what you have and remember the main focus is to teach music to your students and not about the "stuff."

Being a juggler is now part of your job

Congratulations. Not only are you now a music teacher, but also a juggler. You probably didn't know that right? I'm not referring to you actually juggling balls or pins, but your school day. Obviously, you know about the teaching part of your job, but there is truly so much more that will occur during your workday that you'll sometimes not know how to fit it all in.

The first thing you're juggling in your school life is the teaching aspect of things. As an elementary music teacher, you'll be teaching a combination of anywhere from Pre-K to 6th grades. You might also be the middle and/or choir director or band director too if you're in a smaller district. You may also also have a 4th-5th grade honor choir or a drum or Orff ensemble as well.

One of the things throughout your school day you'll notice right away is how your schedule jumps around a lot from an upper grade to a lower grade. It then continues to go back and forth like that all day like a seesaw. You set out what you need for a 1st-grade class, then 5th-grade comes in next, so you need to completely change your mindset and teaching materials for them. It takes a while to get used to, but once you figure out your schedule, you'll get the hang of how much prep and clean up time you need between each class you see.

While you're at school, you're not just going to be juggling teaching and everything that falls into that bucket but will also be planning each week. You sit down before or after school or during your plan time to get some actual planning done, but then you're either interrupted by another teacher, an unexpected meeting or assembly is called, or you're behind in other work that needs to get done. So, what ends up happening is you either rush to plan for the following week or end up needing to take work home. Remember, this is your first year of teaching, so this is the hardest year of planning you'll have. It's going to take a while to figure out your lesson plan format, what curriculum map to use, what exactly to put in your lesson plans, and how much or how little to plan each week.

During your school day, you'll also need to make copies and fill out field trip forms, create sub plans, arrange bars on your mallet instruments, and set up between each class. Then, you'll plan out your programs, and sometimes laminate bulletin boards. Finding the time to do all of this takes consistent effort. You'll figure out a system that works for you, where you're not being pulled in a million different directions. Then, keep doing that to alleviate some of the stress you might be feeling.

Another part of the elementary music teacher juggle during your first year is the fact that you'll need to be creative with finding time for bathroom breaks and to eat lunch. "But wait, aren't I given a lunch break?" That's a fantastic question and one I asked myself many times. You see, any time I would sit down to eat my lunch, a teacher or student would need something or a parent would stop in to have a chat. I had to get some tasks done (see the section right above this one) or I would fall behind. Did this always happen? Of course not! But, I knew if I needed my plan time to actually plan (yeah right), I would need to finish some of my juggling responsibilities during my lunch break. Lunch would sometimes consist of me eating while walking or working.

Now, as for bathroom breaks, your breaks throughout the day are when you'll need to find the time to go. Long gone are your glory days of being able to go to the restroom any time your body signaled it needed to go. You'll eventually get the hang of when you can sneak in a quick break, but at first, it will definitely be a huge surprise to you.

You might feel judged for being the new teacher

As a new teacher, I remember feeling judged some days for being new. There were teachers who honestly didn't think I knew what I was doing and compared me to how THEY felt as a new teacher. This is unfair in so many ways. Yes, things will be hard. Of course, things will take time for you to learn how to do things. You're going to have days that feel like a train wreck. But, your experience gets to be exactly that... YOUR experience.

Listen to advice from seasoned teachers, but still remember that you're you. Every single teacher has started as a new teacher. They may have just forgotten what it was like, because it may have been so long ago. Also, if they do remember their experience, they are probably trying to be helpful with not wanting you to make the same mistakes they did.

You're already going to be feeling uncertain, unsure, and like you don't know what you're doing some days. Can I let you in on a little secret? Even the most seasoned of teachers with 30 years of experience under their belt still feel this way some days. They've just learned how to adapt quickly and keep moving forward, which you eventually will learn to do too! I want you to also not compare your beginning with someone else's middle or end. They ALL started right where you're at and it's taken years of experience, perseverance, and trial and error to get where they're at today.

Some of the best teachers I've mentored in person and online have been first-year teachers. You come to the table with fresh ideas and new perspectives. There's a joy that exudes from first-year teachers because you're so excited to begin teaching. Although the teachers with years of experience have that going for them, a lot of the times they are the ones feeling the burnout big time. Gone are the days where they've just completed their student teaching experience and are beginning a new career.

So, please remember this as you begin your new teaching endeavor. Come to school with fresh ideas and perspectives that are truly your own. The education world needs what you have and there is absolutely no one who can teach music like you can. You have a unique and one of a kind personality and skill sets that set you apart from any other teacher. If you feel judged or looked down upon because you're young, keep your head up. Prove to these other teachers that you're passionate about what you're doing. Show them through your actions and not your words. Then, just watch what happens the first time one of their students shows back up to their classroom with a huge smile on their face singing their hearts out.

Chapter 4: What you need to know about teaching music

There are tons of interruptions

When I became an elementary music teacher, I had no idea the amount of interruptions I would deal with every day. Of course, there are certain days where things flow smoothly and your day seems to just coast on by. But, then there are other days where it feels like the sky is falling, your schedule is in disarray, and like you taught a total of 10 minutes of music that day.

The first type of interruption you have is from the students in your classroom. The types of interruptions you experience can range from students talking out, getting up to blow their nose, playing an instrument when their hands should be in their lap, bothering the student next to them, or not walking to their seat. One of the other interruptions no one ever told me about is that there will be students who will have accidents (of the pee kind) right in the middle of your music room floor.

It's hard to know what to do with the rest of the class when one of these interruptions comes from one of your students. You don't want to embarrass the child or call them out in front of everyone. But, if a child isn't following procedures, it is ok to pull them to the side to remind them of your expectations and procedures.

Then, there are the school-wide interruptions. These consist of fire, tornado, or intruder on campus drills, assemblies, classes being out for a field trip, the intercom going off constantly, your phone ringing, and your administrator or another teacher popping into your room to "have a quick chat." You may have one or more of these types of interruptions on any given day.

Just knowing, realizing, and accepting that interruptions will happen throughout your day is important. Like I said, each day will look different, but knowing that the crazy days will come helps your mindset and keeps you moving forward in your day. If you're a super planner like me, be ok with your schedule being out of whack for a class period or two. Also know that if a class gets behind or misses a song or two, you can easily get them back on track.

Identifying your teaching style takes time

If you took the traditional route in becoming an elementary music teacher, you more than likely took one class that went over the different teaching styles. In your elementary music methods course, it skimmed over the different methods and how you might teach them. You learned what you could do, but had no idea how you were supposed to choose what to use exactly. Guess what? This is the way the majority of elementary music teachers have felt.

To be honest, that's where I learned what my teaching style was the most. I'm a visual learner, so being able to actually go into a real classroom to observe a real teacher and real students was glorious. I got tons of ideas, took lots of notes, and started processing what I wanted to do and what I knew I definitely didn't want to do. But, the idea of all the different teaching methods and how to choose what to use was mind-boggling to me. It wasn't until my third year of teaching that I truly felt comfortable in my own classroom and fell into my teaching style. It just took me getting in there and doing it, and a whole lot of trial and error.

If you're reading this chapter, you might be past your first year of teaching (or maybe you're right smack dab in the middle of it.) That means, you've experienced the "what is my teaching style" confusion that comes right along with being a music teacher. You were pretty sure you had it all figured out in year one. Then, year two hit and you thought, "well maybe not so much." Then, each year you find that you're still slowly figuring out what your teaching style truly is.

You see, it takes more time than you think it does to find your style of teaching music. It's a process for sure. To me, your teaching style is where the teaching method(s) you choose to present music from, your personal musicianship and experiences that led you to be a music teacher, and what your students need from you collide. When you combine all three of these things and bring them to the front of mind each day in your classroom, you end up becoming exactly the music teacher your students need.

How do you choose what teaching method(s) to teach from? The first thing to do is to ask other music teachers. When you're first starting out, you won't know other music teachers to ask. But, reach out to music education majors you went to school with, ask the other music teachers you slowly meet in your district or at workshops, or even reach out to your college professors. They may tell you to refer to your elementary music methods book, which isn't a bad idea actually.

Speaking of workshops, go to as many as you can. Listen to guest presenters who are experts in the music education field. A lot of these workshops will cover anything from Kodaly, Orff, Dalcroze Eurhythmics, Feierabend, Gordon Music Theory, and many more. As I began going to workshops, this is where I realized I'm a combo platter type of teacher. What does this mean? Well, it means that I liked to pull from a lot of different teaching methods. I really don't identify with just one. You might lean more towards one or the other, or you might work in a school district that prefers a certain method. It truly doesn't matter what any other music teacher is doing, because you get to choose what you feel comfortable teaching from. Just do your research, attend training, and figure out what approach meets your musicianship and personality and then do it with confidence.

Your musicianship should continue into your classroom. I see so many music teachers who stop singing for fun or playing their instrument just for the joy of things when they begin teaching their students. It's important for a few reasons you don't allow this to happen. Your musicianship is what helped create you into the music teacher you are. It's part of what made you want to become a music teacher in the first place. Think about your experiences with music. What made you want to pursue music as a child? Who inspired you? What experience caused you to want to teach music to others?

For me, I'm a classically trained pianist. At the age of 6, I came home from school and learned the melody to "Jolly Old St. Nicholas" after hearing my homeroom teacher play it for my class that day. I went on to also play clarinet and played both instruments through middle school, high school, and college. As you can see, I'm an instrumentalist. I LOVE teaching instruments, and actually thought I'd be a band director before falling in love with elementary music. Therefore, I love the Orff approach because of being able to create music, play music, and move to music with my students. But, I also love the Kodaly method because all of my years of piano theory led me to know teaching students music in a sequential order is so important.

Of course, I didn't know what teaching method to use or what my teaching style was right off the bat, but I quickly realized the importance of teaching to what my students needed. What I thought I would do, and what I wrote down as my philosophy of education, wasn't what I actually did at all. I remember trying to mimic what I observed other teachers doing. I would also come back to my school from workshops and try to teach new lessons I had learned the exact same way the presenter did. But, can I let you in on a little secret? That didn't work... not even a little bit.

My students needed me to be me. They needed me to bring my musical experiences and to use my own teaching style. When I was trying to be someone I wasn't, it was almost like I was teaching someone else's students. Then, when I realized what my students needed, focused on teaching them, and worked on forming relationships (which we'll discuss more in chapter 5), that's when things fell into place.

Choosing songs to teach is no easy feat

When I started my first teaching position, all I had at my disposal were some old textbooks. As I began looking through these textbooks, I realized that there were more songs included than I could possibly get through in a school year. Then, after eventually investing in more resources, I had more songs added to the list of what I could teach. How was I supposed to know what song to teach when? Was I supposed to get through every song in all the resources?

I quickly realized that I was stressing myself out trying to get through all the songs, instead of just focusing on teaching music. Yes, although there is so much I could teach doesn't mean I have to get through everything. This is something I definitely wasn't told in college. In my head, I thought I would be handed a curriculum on a golden platter and just know what to teach each day. Boy, was I ever wrong.

Never in a million years did I think that I might literally start out with just some old textbooks. I'm truly grateful I had these books and can't imagine how much more overwhelmed I would've been if I had started out with nothing at all. These old textbooks contained a treasure trove of content and I was able to pull so much out of them.

I remember sitting on the floor in my living room while scattering the resources I had accumulated all around me. Then, I got to work deciding what each grade level needed to learn and a curriculum map was created. After that, I slowly started making my way through all my resources and typed a list of what songs could be used for the different teaching standards. Then, the other songs that could also be used for that standard got added to the list under that topic. I became organized and my life became a whole lot easier when it came to lesson planning the next school year.

There are truly so many amazing songs to teach in elementary music. That's what makes the decision on what to choose so difficult. You don't want your students to miss out on any amazing songs. But, here's what I want you to remember. As long as they're getting a great music education, that's the main goal. It's about quality over quantity. When you focus on teaching music with quality songs, they're going to excel. But, here's the other thing. Remember that list of songs I discussed making? The awesome thing about being a music teacher is you can change what you do.

You might find that you're starting to get bored teaching the same content year in and year out. If so, that's why the list of songs is there. If you're working on singing in a round, you might have 10-25 songs on your list to choose from. If you've done the same five rounds for the last three years, then plug in different rounds next school year. Your students moving from second to third grade won't know that they've missed out on the song "Kookaburra" if you choose not to do it this time around. Remember, it's your classroom and changing things up from time to time is completely fine!

Making your music classroom inclusive to all learners is crucial

You might feel somewhat prepared to teach any child that comes into the music room. But then you get a child who needs extra support, accommodations, or modifications and may feel stuck. That's okay to feel this way. If you've never taught special-needs learners before, you can't just expect to know what to do. When you began teaching music to your students who are typical learners, you probably didn't quite know what you were doing either. With each new challenge presented to you as a music educator, it takes time, consistency, and patience to learn how to best achieve greatness.

As an educator, it's so important that you include all learners. You have kids with all kinds of different giftings and abilities coming through your doors. There are kids who need more support than others, some who are gifted, and others who have special needs. It's so hard to figure out who needs what from you. But, you're more than capable of helping each and every student thrive in your music classroom.

The classroom and resource teachers at your school are more than willing to help give you the right adaptations that a certain child needs. You just have to be willing to ask for help. Look at a child's IEP, 504 plan, or behavior plan to see what accommodations and modifications are already in place. Sometimes this information is given to you and the special education team at your school is great about providing services and support for what to do in the music room, and sometimes you'll need to be proactive in obtaining this information on your own.

When you know a child is coming into the music room with a specific disability or disorder, do your own research as well. Learn about ways you can help that child be successful when it comes to learning music. Every child can and should learn music. It's not a matter of if they can, but how can they. Read and educate yourself, go to specific training, listen to podcasts, and make sure you are doing everything you can to help kids learn music, no matter their ability.

In the music classroom, make sure your classroom is inclusive. Re-evaluate the way you're grouping kids together. If an aide is coming to the music room, give them specific ways they can help you in supporting a particular child. Think of ways you can accommodate the music experience for special needs learners. Stay patient with these kiddos, because they really do want to learn. It takes lots of consistency when creating and implementing lesson plans, coming up with a classroom management plan, and learning the ropes of teaching music, the same goes for knowing how to adapt your teaching to reach every single child you get the pleasure of teaching.

Creating a diverse classroom environment matters

Your school has a variety of different cultures and races represented. It's so important you're aware of the students you're teaching because you need to make sure all students feel seen, heard, and understood. They need to be able to feel comfortable in your music room and to hear, learn, sing, and play songs that represent their culture. Just like you spend time researching ways to accommodate the special learners in your classroom, you need to do the same when it comes to making sure the music you're teaching is relevant and meaningful to all students.

What I learned at various workshops was amazing. But, I knew it couldn't just be a cookie-cutter approach and that I needed to take what I learned and adapt it to meet my students where they were at. There were songs and activities I chose to do that were a complete and total failure. If this has happened to you, make it into a learning experience for yourself. A lot of teaching, as you've probably already learned, is done by trial and error. If something doesn't resonate with your students, then think through what can go better or if you need to make different song choices.

How can you make sure you're representing every child in your classroom? The best way to do this is by choosing a mixture of songs, activities, stories, composers, instruments, and movement activities. You see your students for 36 weeks. During those weeks of school, make every minute count. Vary up what you do and be ok with thinking outside of the box.

With my black students, I taught about the different musical careers they could have, we composed music using hip hop beats, learned about black musical artists and composers, and had days where we listened to their favorite music and evaluated the music together through listening and exploration. But, we also learned about the different cultures from around the world. In fact, we'd cover a different culture or country every month. We read so many books, listened to music, learned songs in other languages, talked about the culture of that particular country and why the music was written. We also discussed what composers came from that country and what students in our class were from that country or culture.

It's also important that kids experience music from cultures other than their own. So many kids are only familiar with music from their own culture. It's the music teacher's job to make sure you're creating various musical avenues and connections for your students.

For some of your kids, this is the first time they'll get to experience any type of music, besides what they experience on the radio, from movies, at live sports events, at church, or somewhere else in their own life. When you bring music to them from around the world, or even from their own culture, you're opening doors for them to explore music in ways they never knew possible. While learning about composing raps, bring in a real rap artist or listen to a clean version of a rap together. When students learn about a mariachi band, try to bring in a member of a band or show the students what the mariachi band looks like via online video. If students are learning about folk music, have them listen to the banjo and talk about what a folk band is. By varying up what music you're not only teaching, but having students listen to, explore, experience, move to, read stories about, and feel, you're helping make the world of music relevant to them.

Students need to also see pictures of people who look like them. When you vary up what music you do, be aware of what bulletin boards and books you're bringing into your classroom as well. Are most of your books of just white kids? Do you have any books with pictures of black or brown children as well? Do the posters in your room represent people with various skin colors? If not, then this is something to definitely think about doing. Remember, it's about knowing what students you're teaching and making sure they feel seen, heard, and valued each and every day.

Putting on a musical performance is a lot of work

When you get into teaching elementary music, you know that putting on performances is definitely a huge part of the job. But, what no one let me in on, is all the things involved with planning and implementing these performances. I had no idea how to put on a performance, what music to choose, where exactly to find music, and realized pretty quickly that I felt like I was in over my head. If it was just about getting my students on the stage to sing and perform beautiful music, I'd be all set. But, I definitely learned that putting on a great performance, especially with the youngest of students, had way more than that involved.

Maybe you can relate to this in one way or another. Maybe you came to elementary music from a secondary position and planning a band or choir concert is quite a bit different. Or maybe you underestimated the amount of time that went into planning and choosing music for your students.

When it comes to planning performances, the first thing I found out was that choosing dates on a calendar mattered a lot. I couldn't just wing it and casually mention we would be having the 2nd-grade program on March 31st. No way! Looking at the school calendar at the end of the school year and getting my program dates on the next school year's calendar was the very first step. You might be at a smaller school and can combine K-1st, 2nd-3rd, and 4th-5th. Or, you might be at a larger school and there is absolutely no way you can do that. Just decide who will be performing together, and get it on the calendar.

After putting on a few performances, I re-evaluated the way I did things. I started hearing from other elementary music teachers about informances. This idea was so appealing to me because I thought it was a fantastic way for students to showcase what they had been working on during our time in music together. It's also something I hadn't learned about in college and therefore didn't even know was a thing! So, I decided for me, I would have some grade levels put on performances for an audience, while other grade levels did informances in our music classroom. This ended up working out well and was a great way to advocate for music education through various means.

You might enjoy putting on performances, or informances, or even musicals. Remember that you get to be completely you in your music room. You're a unique teacher, with a personality all your own, and have your own school dynamics to navigate around. You might have expectations put on you by your administration or you might get to decide how you want to put on music performances at your school. But, the main goal is for students to get the experience of performing for an audience. They gain so much by not just performing, but practicing and discussing audience etiquette, stage presence, and can even do a post-performance assessment.

When you plan for your performances (no matter which one you choose), picking a theme and music to go with that will take some time. There are some great sites (I'm looking at you MusicK8) that provide ready to go program music. I've found some amazing programs on this site and the awesome thing is once the music is purchased, you can use it again in the future. Another great way to put on a performance is to use what students have already learned. If you'll be putting on a Winter program, you know you've already done tons of songs about snowmen and Santa. What better way to put together a program than by using what you've already done?

But in the thick of it all, don't forget about the importance of communicating with the teachers and parents. You need to keep them informed about any dress rehearsals, decorations the students can help make, what the students should wear, or any other pertinent information you think they should know. With the parents, you also need to communicate with them about any special parts their child may have and where to have their child the night of the performance.

It takes time to build your music program

Imagine walking into a music classroom after accepting a new teaching position. Then, you look around slowly and realize there are no instruments or teaching resources, except for one broken hand drum and a set of textbooks that are from 1846. Ok, maybe more like the 1990s. This was my exact experience. In college, I learned about how to teach with the variety of instruments I thought I would have. We talked about using various teaching resources and how the teacher whose position you took over, would be leaving tons of materials behind. Oh yeah, and there would be chairs and a budget to order what I needed. Um... not so much.

To be honest, I was a bit angry and frustrated right at that moment. I wasn't upset at my school, because it hadn't had music for 7 years. I was more irritated that no one had ever told me this could also be a possible scenario. It honestly never went through my mind that I might need to know how to build a music program from scratch.

Maybe you're reading this section and you're slowly nodding your head in agreement. Or, even if you did follow in the footsteps of a music teacher before you, they didn't leave you with much or you've ended up purchasing a ton of resources with your own money. But, you may have walked into a classroom with a great setup and so much support, and if so, I'm so incredibly happy for you.

Whatever situation you find yourself in, it takes time to build your music program up. It takes time to get what instruments, materials, and resources you need for your classroom. Make a list of what you want and need. Then, figure out where the money will be coming from to get those items. Will it come from your PTA? Do you have any type of budget? Are you going to use Donors Choose? Can you apply for a grant? Don't overwhelm yourself trying to get everything right away, but do it slowly over time.

It also takes time to shape your music program into what you want it to be. The good thing about having "stuff" for your classroom is that is one less thing you need to think about. But, the tough thing is you're going to be constantly feeling like you're being compared to that previous teacher. It takes a while to move out of that shadow and to show everyone at school it's ok to do things your way. Each year, you'll break down that unspoken wall that seems to be there, and you'll establish your presence as THE music teacher. I've mentioned this before, but after your third year of teaching, you'll find your confidence and will grow into who you are as a teacher. Just remember to give yourself grace and to keep taking steps forward.

Also, I want to let you know that no one knows your students like you do. When you see a classroom set up a certain way, would that necessarily work for your classroom? How do your students learn best? The materials and songs you've learned at conferences and workshops are so amazing. But, how many times have you sat in a session and thought to yourself, "well this is an amazing activity, but my students wouldn't respond to it this way." Thinking this way is the sign of you being an amazing teacher. Why? I feel like when you think through activities and about your students, you're teaching to the students you have. You're wanting to make teaching music as relevant as you can. So, take what you learn and adapt it to fit your teaching demographic, school setting, personal teaching style, and expectations set upon you by your principal.

Lesson planning and teaching lessons don't always go hand in hand

Sitting down each week to create your lesson plans takes a lot of thought and time. You get so excited while planning to implement these lessons with your students. But, sometimes lessons just don't go as planned. There are a lot of factors that play into this. You have classroom and school-wide interruptions, and individual students needing something at different times. Not to mention the fact that if there was a full moon the night before, class parties happening, or if it's a rainy day, you might not be able to teach what you had planned to.

This used to stress me out so badly. My type-A personality wanted to have all my ducks lined up in a very neat and orderly row. What happened some days was more like frogs hopping around my classroom and things felt out of my control. I had to learn that it's ok to let go of those super tough expectations I had put on myself. Learning to stay flexible and to roll with the punches was what was needed some days.

You see... while preparing to become a teacher, you learn all about lesson planning. You learn what to include, what different formats you might use, where to insert your objectives and standards, and all about assessment. But, the thing that they don't tell you is that you can have the most well designed and put together lesson plan in the entire world, but you might not be able to use it. It doesn't matter how neat and tidy things look on paper if in person it's messy and chaotic.

I learned that my best lessons were the ones where I left enough space for those unexpected interruptions. I stopped overplanning and remembered to also leave enough time in my lesson plans for the students to develop their musical creativity. We also had more time to chat when they entered and exited my classroom as well. A lot of what happens in a music room, as I quickly learned, wasn't just about music.

As a music teacher, you learn to improvise lessons really well too. If you do end up with extra time at the end of the class period, you become an expert at making things up as you go. You also develop so many filler activities that will keep your students engaged through moving, stories, fun games, and extension activities. Some of my favorite lessons are the ones I just kind of threw together last minute. If a class wasn't able to focus on what I was teaching from the lesson plan I created, I became ok switching things up. Knowing when a lesson plan just isn't going to work, and also realizing you can revisit it later is so important.

Music education will continue changing every year

Think back to your elementary music class from when you were a kid. What do you remember? Was it anything like elementary music is now? No way! For me, my music teacher had one of those handheld bells where one hand hits the top of it to make the sound come out. When she wanted my class to get quiet, she would ring that thing over and over. This is definitely not a classroom management strategy I used in my classroom. For the music part of things, I remember just sitting and singing. We really didn't do much else than that.

Now, elementary music classrooms everywhere are filled with not just sitting and singing, but movement, so many instruments, puppets, scarves, Smartboards, Chromebooks, iPads, books, and so many other amazing materials. Besides the stuff, kids are doing a lot more moving and less sitting in the music room.

I think having education continue to evolve and change is a good thing. As the times change, education needs to as well. The kids of today are growing up in the age of technology and it's up to educators to keep up. What you learned while getting your education degree, might be way different than what you're actually doing in your classroom now. It feels like every day you have new expectations, requirements, or some kind of new technology to learn how to implement with your students.

Although it can be stressful having education changing all the time, it's so important that you don't stay stuck in your ways. Some teachers don't want to learn new ways of doing things, because they've simply been doing it the same way for so many years. I totally get that. Remember, I already told you I'm a creature of habit and like to stay organized. But, it's so important that music educators have a growth mindset just like you're always telling your students to do. Their minds are constantly being molded and stretched to learn new things.

Chapter 5: What you need to know about classroom management

There's a lot more to classroom management than just managing

As teachers we all know the importance of classroom management. I don't know about you, but learning about it being needed in my classroom is all I learned about it. My college was small and a lot of the time the music education majors were lumped into the education classes with the other education majors. I remember loving my classroom management class. My professor did a fantastic job breaking down the do's and don'ts of what to do in a classroom setting. But, it was so generic. Nowhere in that class did we cover specific examples for what to do in an actual music classroom.

I moved on to teaching and met my mentor teacher. She was a great teacher but taught 3rd grade. So here I was once again getting advice from a non-musical person. The advice I received from her was to be super strict upfront, and then I can let my guard down. So, that's what I did. It became all about rules and procedures (which I'll get into more in a bit) and I thought I had finally figured it out. But, something was missing.

I wasn't enjoying this approach at all. I didn't want to feel like I was a dictator and the kids were just doing what I asked of them because I was so strict. Classroom management should encompass procedures and expectations of course, but it should also be about building relationships with students too. A lot of it also has to do with the fact that class time needs to keep moving, so there's not a lot of down time for kids to get distracted, bother their neighbor, or talk out of turn. We'll get into all of that in a minute, but before we do, I want you to realize that classroom management is about a lot more than just "managing."

Classroom management isn't a one size fits all approach. Just because you see something is working at one school, doesn't mean it will work at yours. I feel like classroom management is a completely individual decision. What is your personality? What are you comfortable with when it comes to class and individual rewards and consequences? Are there ideas you've just been so excited to implement in your classroom? When choosing what classroom management approach to take, just remember that it isn't as scary as it sounds. You are more than capable of being able to teach music to your students day in and day out, without constantly feeling like you're just dealing with behavior issues.

Setting up your classroom matters

Setting up your classroom is a huge part of classroom management. Strategically planning where to put chairs, what to hang on the wall, how much open space to have in your classroom, and where to seat your students all matters more than you think. You've probably seen so many amazing music classrooms, whether you're a new teacher or not. Have you noticed anything special? No two classrooms are set up exactly the same. Why is this? Well, I've said it once and I'll say it again. You are uniquely you. The way you set up YOUR classroom is completely up to what you're wanting to do, your teaching style, and what your students need.

So, how does setting up your classroom contribute to a classroom management plan? Think about going to someone else's house. You walk in for the first time and don't really know where to sit or what you're allowed to touch. Also, if the house is really messy or unorganized, it makes you feel a little uncomfortable. If your students are allowed to just walk into the classroom and sit wherever and there's no order in your classroom, that will cause confusion. Students need to be aware of where to sit and when they're supposed to do it. We'll get more into procedures in another section, but for now, let's focus on your classroom and how to set it up for maximum effectiveness.

In your own living space at home, do you like lots of colors or to keep things simple? Do you have a lot on your walls or just a few pieces? A lot of who you are combined with your teaching style we've talked so much about will help determine how much and what to put on your walls in your classroom. On your walls, no matter how much you want to include, make sure you have defined spaces. When I began setting up my classroom space, I just kind of went for a colorful approach. But, I didn't really think about what I was putting on my walls. There wasn't a rhyme or reason to it. Then, I realized everything I put on my classroom walls needs to serve a purpose.

The first thing to consider is to have a word wall. This is where you can post any bulletin boards or musical terms you want your students to remember. They need to be hung up where students can visibly see them. Your visual learners will especially appreciate this wall. Most of the time this wall can be somewhere where when the students are leaving your classroom, they can see it and look it over. You might even have space next to it where the kids can write out on note cards or sticky notes about what they learned that day.

Your other walls can contain motivational posters or quotes by famous composers and musicians. You might also put a bulletin board outside of your room and/or inside of your classroom that changes depending on the composer, culture, or instrument of the month. Then, you can also have a "get to know me" section on a wall for students to see who you are with pictures of your family and friends.

The next thing to think about when setting up your classroom is the actual stuff going into your classroom. This will be any chairs or other seating you want, a floor carpet, your desk, resources of course, large and small instruments, student computers, iPads, and student books. You may have something else you want to add to the list, but these are the staples you should consider. Every personality and teaching style is different, depending on who you are. Wait, have you heard that before? Of course you have! So, when I talk about where to put all the things, please remember to do what you're comfortable with and to keep in mind how you want to teach. The main goal is for your students to learn music in an effective and productive way. You don't get to see your students very often, so when you do, make every moment count.

Have procedures for everything

What procedures do you already have in place? How many do you go over with your students? How often do you review the procedures? These are all questions to consider and to revisit often. I like to compare procedures to a machine. If you think about what a machine needs to function, it's a whole lot of moving parts, right? If there's even one nut or bolt missing, the machine won't function the way it was created to. When it comes to procedures, if there's a piece not in place, your class time won't run nearly as smoothly as it could.

When it comes to procedures, I thought I had the right ones in place during my first couple of years. There were the enter and exit procedures, instrument procedures (sort of), and all the "rules" procedures. But, what I failed to realize was that these were just scraping the surface of what I would truly need to have set in place in my music classroom. Leaving school most days, I would wonder what I was doing wrong. It felt like a puzzle piece was missing (or a bolt) and I couldn't put my finger on it. I was tired of the talking, the not listening, the breakdown in transitions, the not following instructions, and not being able to get through a full lesson plan. This was on my shoulders to figure out, and I was determined to do so.

I went back to the drawing board and identified what was breaking down in my music room and realized what was missing was procedures. I didn't have enough. So, more procedures began being added. Everything began to flow smoother and I was actually able to start teaching more music! Was each day perfect? Of course not! It never will be. But, the good days started to outweigh the hard (because there are never bad days, only days you can learn and grow from.)

Think about what goes on in your music room for those 30-55 minutes. From the moment your students step through your classroom door, what are they doing during each moment? Each class period will look different depending on what content you're teaching and what activities you have planned. So much goes on in such a short period of time. No wonder music teachers leave school exhausted each day. You pour your heart out and physically and mentally give to your students each day. But, there is a way to make sure you don't constantly need to say "be quiet" or "stay in your seat", and that's by having procedures in place.

Here are the procedures that will help you and your students have the best music class experience each time they come into your room:

- How do you want them to come into the music room?
- Where are their seats and how are they supposed to walk to them?
- Are they supposed to be doing a body percussion warm-up right when they get to their seats?

- What happens next? Do students know what to expect, where to look for instructions, or how to listen to you giving them instructions?

- If it's time to get an instrument or walk to a large instrument, how do they walk to them?

- What do they do once they have an instrument? You can tell them to keep their hands in their laps and to have their eyes on you or say something like, "play before I say, I'll take your instrument away."

- When you teach a new song, what do students do with their voices and bodies? Are they supposed to echo sing after you or listen to you sing while patting or walking to the steady beat?

- After students learn a new song, what happens next? Do they know what to do or how to listen to instructions given? What happens if they talk?

- Do you have individual and class rewards and consequences in place?

- Are you spending too much time giving instructions instead of showing students what to do instead then quickly moving to the lesson procedure?

- Do you keep class time moving and not give students a lot of down time to talk?

- When it comes to doing a movement activity, do students know the procedures for listening, learning, and implementing?
- With partner or small group activities, do you choose this or do they choose who they're with?
- While working on a program or performance, what are the procedures for this? What are your expectations for students?
- Do students know when it's time to stop and clean up? What are your procedures for this? How do you close out class time?
- If a child has a question, what are they supposed to do? What about when it comes to needing to blow their nose or go to the restroom?

As you can see, there are so many procedures you can have in place. You may have more to add to this list, and I have way more I could've listed here as well. But, when learning to implement procedures in your classroom, know that it's better to have too many than not enough. When students know what to expect and feel a sense of comfort in knowing you're the leader, they'll rise to the occasion and will feel confident in your classroom.

Class time needs to keep moving along

One of the most effective classroom management strategies is to keep class time moving along. This is definitely one of those easier said than done types of things. There is so much to teach, and so little time to do it in. You see your students, on average, about 45 minutes once a week. But, you also have tons of objectives to cover and curriculum resources to get through. There's so much to consider when thinking about how to plan and implement the lessons. One of the factors we're not told to think about while in college is how much to teach in the time that our students are in the music room. It feels like a big guessing game at times.

Creating smooth transitions helps students stay aware of what's coming up next. Your transitions will look different each day, depending on what you're teaching or what you have planned. Some great ideas for helping students transition between activities or to enter and exit your classroom include walking to the beat while singing a song, you playing a rhythm on the hand drum, giving students different action words to move to like skip, tiptoe, move like a snake, sway to the beat, etc. The main thing to keep in mind is to keep your directions clear, and for students to know exactly what to do and what you expect during each moment of your music room. This goes right back to having a procedure for everything.

That combined with you having clear transitions will help your class time to keep moving along smoothly.

But, what about the days full of interruptions? Every day won't look chaotic, but unfortunately, some of them will. How you handle these interruptions, while still continuing to teach music, is what music teachers need to learn how to do. This definitely is one of those things that isn't taught in college. There isn't a class called "How to Handle the Child Peeing on Your Classroom Floor 101." So, unfortunately, you become a music teacher and begin to realize you can plan the best lessons in the world, but you'll only get through about ¾ of them.

It's hard to keep class time moving when you get interrupted all day.

Here's an example of how a day might play out for you. Right when you begin your lesson, your principal walks into your classroom to tell you something. That eats up two minutes. Right after she/he leaves, you start teaching again. Then, the intercom goes off and little Billy needs to gather his stuff to leave for a dentist appointment. Alright. Now, you're really going to get started. Umm... why are students scooting away from Amy? Uh oh. She had an accident and pee is now everywhere. Welp, time to call the janitor. You scoot everyone away and the mess gets cleaned up. Amy gets sent to the office to get some clean pants. You finally are able to teach about 15 minutes of your lesson and then a fire alarm goes off. Wait, was this planned? You can't remember, but have to stop what you're doing to take the class to the designated spot outside. By the time you get back to your classroom, it's time to send that class back to their regular classroom and your next class is waiting to come in.

When there are interruptions from a single child or the kind that disrupts the entire class, have some ideas in mind for how you can try to keep instruction going. You've already taught the students so many songs, so play music and have students sing along to it. Or, you can call a child to the front of the class to lead everyone in some echo rhythm patterns. Another idea is to play music and have students creatively move to it. If they've already been doing creative movement in your music class, this will be like second nature to them. Is there a game or activity you can put on the Smartboard the students can actively engage with? Is there a GoNoodle you can play that they can dance along to? If students can't go to their regular seats, can you line them up in a straight line to play rhythm telephone?

There are so many ideas you can have ready to go when, not if, the interruptions come. Be clear with students ahead of time about what your procedures will be for the different interruptions that might come up. Then, when they occur, although students may be caught off guard, they'll know what to do. This is just another thing that needs to be planned out and thought of ahead of time so that all of you are ready for when it happens. Of course, there is a huge difference between the younger and older kiddos. With the littles, you might have to adjust your "backup" plans accordingly. But also, please remember that if a class ends up getting off task due to the different circumstances happening that are out of your control, know that you can get them back on track. If you can't get them back on track that class period, make a note of it, and try again the next time you see them. All you can do is your best. If you've tried to keep class time moving along, even on one of those crazy chaotic days, and you feel like nothing you tried worked, then let it go. These days are going to come. It happens to every teacher. Instead of focusing on what went wrong, use it as a lesson to help propel you forward, so when the situations arise again in the future, you'll be a bit more prepared for whatever may come your way.

Give it time and don't give up

The thing with classroom management I wish someone had told me about, is that you have to give it time. If you try something and notice it just isn't working like you want it to, don't give up too soon. Also, what works with one class won't work with another. A lot of classroom management is done by trial and error. You may have a classroom management approach ready to try out, and then notice it doesn't go over well with your students. Does this mean you failed? Of course not! It just means you need to try something else.

How often do you need to try something new? Well, that depends on several factors. How long have you been at your school? Do the students know you well or are they just getting to know you? Have you gone over the procedures and expectations once or many times? Were your students used to another classroom management system and are now learning a new approach? Are your expectations clear and follow through on negative and positive consequences consistent?

These are all questions you need to ask yourself. Then, once you've thought about these things, keep in mind that you can't give up. Whether you're trying out a new classroom management system or you've been doing the same thing for years, you just can't get frustrated. Are there days you want to throw in the towel and be done? Of course. Classroom management is one of the hardest, if not THE hardest part, of being a music teacher. In a perfect world, music teachers would just be able to show up and teach music. All of this managing a classroom stuff is hard work!

Every teacher at some point in their career has struggled with classroom management with at least one class or student. The approach that works for one teacher won't necessarily work for you. That's why if you try to do something because you've seen it work great with another teacher's students and it doesn't work well for you, it's because that teacher isn't you. They don't have the students you have and aren't teaching at your school. Of course, it's okay to try something you've learned, but it's also alright to make classroom management work for you and your students.

Whether you're trying something new, changing things up for one or a few classes, or are continuing what you've been doing, remember to give it time. It's kind of like a puzzle. Certain pieces fit together, yet you've tried to match pieces over and over until you find the right combination. The same goes for classroom management. Eventually, you'll find what sticks and things will become easier. All of a sudden, you ARE able to teach more music to your students, because you found the right approach that works. So, hang in there, keep trying, don't give up, and know that patience is key.

It's okay to change things up every year

We've already discussed how it's important to give classroom management time to work. But, I also want you to realize that it's ok to change things up every year. Your personality, what your students need, your administrator's expectations of you, and your teaching style all play a part in this decision. You might be one of those teachers who like to change up lesson plans and do a new rotation of songs and activities each year. Or, you might be the kind of teacher who likes to do the same things with each grade level every year. There isn't a right or wrong choice here.

Just like lesson planning, the same goes for your classroom management approach. You're going to hear so many different opinions coming your way of what other music teachers are doing with their students. You might also hear them say they change things up a lot or that their system is the magic solution. But, this just isn't true. What works for one teacher won't work for another.

Maybe you do find yourself wanting to change things up every year. For you, it's so exciting trying new approaches and for your students to never know what to expect when they come through your doors. Or, maybe you like things to stay the same and you're a creature of habit. You have your system in place and don't want to mess with introducing something new all the time. But whatever camp you find yourself in, know that it's ok to change things up every year. You don't have to, but if you choose to do this, your students will adapt and adjust as you go.

Building relationships with your students is the key to success

The one thing I wish was emphasized more while learning about classroom management is the fact that building relationships with students is one of the most important things. There can be all the procedures and classroom management techniques in the world put in place, but without relationship building and truly getting to know your students, it won't matter. Yes, your students may follow the rules and know what to expect when they're in the music room, but that might be all they do. When it comes to talking to you and trusting you as an adult in their life, they need that relational aspect as well.

I was never taught about the importance of building relationships with my students. No one ever told me that classroom management was more than just rules and expectations. The fact that I would have students who went through real trauma in their lives and who needed me to be more than a music teacher was never brought up. Kids are facing so much more now than we could ever possibly imagine. They're dealing with such big emotions at such a young age.

As an elementary music teacher, you have to be a bit more creative with forming relationships with your students. Before school starts, stand in the hallway and say hi to the kids or give them a high five. Go into the cafeteria every once and a while and sit down next to a group of your students and just talk about whatever they want. After school, chat with the kids in the bus rider or car lines. During class, leave open space while you're planning your lessons to have conversations with your students. This might be as they're walking in, between activities, around the song or lesson you're teaching, or as they're lining up to leave.

However you choose to form relationships with your students is your choice. Just make this a goal of yours and you realize how vital it is to not only gaining but keeping your students trust day in and day out. They need you to be a role model and to see you as not just a music teacher, but also a person. Be vulnerable and real with them. Let your guard down from time to time. Show your human emotions and have conversations around that.

As you already know, there are some days you won't teach a lot of music. There are days that your students, or a certain student, will need you to be there for them as a mentor. As a teacher, it's important to notice if a certain student, group of kids, or a whole class is having a rough day. Getting to know your students will help you to decipher what the needs are in your classroom every class period of each day.

Chapter 6: What you need to know about school dynamics

Stay on good terms with the secretary and janitor

I was in my Secondary Classroom Methods class in college and my professor Dr. Wilson said, "The main two people you need to have a good relationship with at your school are the secretary and the janitor." I heard him say that and didn't quite get what he meant. Of course, I would have a good relationship with them. I strive to be kind and respectful to everyone I meet. But, why would being on good terms with these two people matter so much?

After beginning teaching, I quickly realized what Dr. Wilson meant. I wasn't even through my first full week of teaching when a student threw up in my classroom, I needed an updated list of the classes, my computer wasn't working right, and a couple of my lights went out. What a way to start the week right? Guess who I needed to help me solve these problems? You guessed it... the secretary and the janitor.

These two people are utilized in your school building more than anyone else. There are so many teachers, support staff, administrators, and even parents vying for their attention every single day. Not only that, they have also a to-do list a mile long, so being interrupted for unexpected issues or problems isn't ideal. They're aware that these problems will arise and are used to dealing with them, but it's so hard to meet the needs of so many different people all the time.

I remember the janitor stopping by my room just to see if I needed anything at times. He told me of certain teacher's classrooms he didn't like to go in due to the lack of respect. When push came to shove if it came down to me or another teacher needing something at the same time, who do you think he chose? Of course, always be kind and don't just be nice so you're put at the front of the list. That's not what I'm saying at all. What I am saying is when you're nice to others and show mutual respect, you'll get that respect right back.

The other person I've already mentioned that is so important to get to know is the school secretary. Most of the time, the secretary is doing all the office administrative tasks, as well being the technology coordinator for the building. That means, when it comes to scheduling field trips, needing any technology fixed, handling class lists, and keeping track of funds to order supplies for your music room, this will be the person you need to have a great rapport with. Value your school secretary. They are literally the backbone of your school and you'll need their help more than you know.

Relationships with the other teachers takes time

Relationships take time and are hard work. Just like it takes 3 years to establish your teaching style and to feel comfortable with who you are as a teacher, the same goes for getting to know the other teachers you work with. When it comes to forming relationships with your teacher colleagues, it depends on several factors.

One of those factors is your personality. If you're more of the quiet and introverted personality, like I am, you'll naturally be shyer and slower to warm up to others. Even though it takes more time, relationships will eventually form as you slowly let your guard down. If you have an extroverted personality, you're able to get to know the other teachers quicker. This doesn't mean that it won't take time for relationships to grow still, but it probably goes at a faster pace for you.

Another factor to consider is that all teachers aren't the same. I mean, we've talked about that in this book over and over again. But, what I mean when it comes to forming relationships is that some teachers you'll click with and get their full support, and others well, not so much. Just like you've been encouraged to use your unique personality in your classroom, the same goes for the other teachers in your school as well. When you throw lots of different personalities and teaching styles into one building, it can get interesting.

Think about friendships in your life right now. More than likely, it took months or years for those friendships to grow and flourish. You had to keep pouring into these friends' lives, showing an interest in what they said, and having conversations with them. Relationships don't just happen overnight or by happenstance. They take consistent effort and work to make sure they last and stand the test of time.

This is the same when it comes to the teachers in your building. Some you connect with on day one, and some will take a much longer time to form a relationship with. Some teachers fully support the music program, and some act like they don't care about anything but you covering their plan time. Some teachers offer you help and support, and others think of you as just a glorified babysitter.

What can you do? Keep showing up and being yourself. Participate in Friday happy hour or sit at different tables during staff meetings (which most of the time have nothing to do with what's happening in the music room.) Offer support and ways to collaborate with what they're doing in their classrooms just like you want them to do for you. Then, remember that the right relationships will blossom, and others will stay cordial. Try to find those two or three teachers who you can rely on, ask questions of, and who are a support system. It's ok not to be "friends" with everyone in your school. But, trying to have good relationships and being kind to everyone you work with is the main goal.

Getting to know your team is important

As the music teacher, your team will look a bit different than the 4th-grade or 2nd-grade teams. Your teaching team usually consists of the art teacher, librarian, computer teacher, P.E. teacher, and the counselor. This combination will look different from school to school, but for the most part, this is who is on your team. It's important to get to know all the teachers and staff in your school building, but especially this team of teachers. Although they don't teach music, these teachers are your biggest supporters and will cheer you on when it feels like no one else is.

You'll need their help from time to time in a lot of different ways. One of those ways is when it comes to students. There are times that no matter what you try with a certain student, they're still a disruption in your classroom. A lot of times, just one tip or suggestion will help you out. The other teacher might share an idea of something they've done with the child that you can implement or tweak to make work in the music room.

These teachers understand the constant ebb and flow to the day and can sympathize about getting classes back to back. They can talk to you about the schedules, about what's working or not working, what they're doing to wrap up a class to get the next class in the room, and what pacing of their lessons look like. Of course, it will look different because of the various subjects taught, but some ideas the other teachers on your team give you will help so much.

When you have a musical performance, these are the teachers who help you out the most. The art teacher volunteers to make decorations and the computer teacher offers to help with the technology side of things. All of the teachers on your team will be there to help get students on and off the risers during a dress rehearsal or to help with whatever it is you need. But on top of that, you also support any school art shows, book fairs, field days, and coding events your school has. You have each other's backs and will be there to support and help each other out with whatever you need.

Give these relationships time to form as well. Pour into these relationships and these teachers will want to pour right back into you. Offer help any time you can, and you'll get the help you need right back. Observe them, ask questions, talk about your struggles and wins, and just be there to encourage each other all school year long.

Parent communication and support matters

When I was in college, I honestly don't remember talking about how much parent communication and support mattered. I knew I would need to talk to the parents about their kids from time to time, and I also knew that my school would have some sort of PTA program, but I never realized how much communicating I would truly be doing. Staying in contact with the parents of your students matters. You keep them up to date about what's happening in regards to any performances coming up, but also want their full support when it comes to what their child is doing in your music room.

Communication with parents will happen in lots of different ways. You sometimes need to talk to them at an in-person conference, while they're picking up their child from school, or on the phone. There are times you need to discuss what's going on with their child both positively and negatively. Call up an unexpecting parent just to let them know their child is doing an amazing job in the music room. Sit in an IEP or behavior plan meeting to find out more about how to best serve a student.

Most of the parents at your school want to support you and your music program. Notice that I said MOST. Just like when dealing with students, there are always certain parents who no matter what you try to do, you just can't please them. They're negative, want things done their way, and will offer suggestions and advice as to how things should be done in your music class. Unfortunately, this is just part of being a teacher.

As for those supportive parents I mentioned earlier, these are your biggest fans and advocates. They are the ones volunteering for anything and everything you need. These are the parents voting at PTA meetings for you to receive funds to purchase new recorders. These are also the parents you contact about their child, who will not hesitate to support you. Know who these parents are and write down their names if needed. You will need parental support from time to time, so having a group of parents you can turn to when you need something is so important.

Every school dynamic is different

Back in chapter 4, we talked about the importance of being yourself and using your unique teaching style. But, you may have noticed that what works at one school doesn't necessarily work at another school. Why? Well, that's because just like no two personalities of music teachers are the same, neither are two schools, the students at that school, or the type of school you're teaching at.

Let's talk about the different types of schools there are first. There are public, charter, and private schools. But, within each of these categories of schools are subcategories. One public or charter school won't look the same as the public or charter school down the street. Then, there are private schools. Just like when discussing public schools, all private schools are different too. But, what's the same is how they are all funded by tuition and private funds. Private schools will sometimes also require that the music teacher prepares music for weekly chapels as well as incorporating more religious music into their curriculum too.

Along with what type of school you teach at, will be the students you teach. Every school will have a different demographic of the student population. You can't walk into a school with a high percentage of black students and expect to just teach them white folk songs. That will not go over well. Trust me, I know from experience. It's VITAL that you teach to your current students, and to change things up if something isn't working. It all goes back to meeting your students where they're at and teaching to the students you have. If lesson plans, songs, and activities worked at one school, but don't go over well with students at another school, it doesn't mean you all of a sudden became a terrible music teacher. It just means that you need to change things up a bit. You can't shove a square peg into a round hole. It's just not going to work.

Every principal, teacher, support staff, parent, and student plays a factor into how the dynamics of your school flows. The expectations in regards to performances, your schedule, how long you see your students, what teaching approach you should use, how much or little parental involvement your school has, if you have a budget or resources, will differ from school to school as well. It takes a while to learn the way your school functions, and what works and doesn't work in regards to teaching music, but you will eventually get it.

Advocating for your music program comes in many different forms

Music advocacy is huge. When there are budget cuts, music programs are a lot of times the first thing to go. It's so sad, to be honest. But, that's why advocating for music education is so important. Maybe you're reading this, and you want to advocate, but just don't know how to. Then, let's discuss the ways you're already advocating right now without even realizing it.

First of all, send home a letter to the parents at the beginning of the school year. Have this same letter hanging up outside your classroom door for anyone and everyone to read as they walk by your room. In the letter, introduce yourself, but also let parents know what their child will be learning in music this year. Tell them how music helps their child learn in other subject areas. Make them aware of the cooperative learning that will take place in your room. Explain what happens when a school doesn't have music and all the ways it helps a child to feel successful. The main goal here is for the parents to know you and why you value music education so very much.

The next way you already advocate for your music program is by teaching your students music day in and day out. Do you know what happens after school? These kids go home to their parents and siblings and start singing the same songs, playing the same games, doing the same dances, or patting the same rhythms they were taught in music class that day. In turn, the parents or grandparents hear, see, and experience what that child learned in music class. They may think back to what they learned in their elementary music class and notice how different it was. But also, they will see the joy on the child's face and will smile seeing this child, who might even be a struggling learner, succeed in music.

Another way you advocate for your music program is by showcasing what the students are working on. You do this by putting on a performance, doing an informance in your classroom, or even inviting the parents and other teachers to stop in from time to time to observe. There are so many times others just aren't aware of what happens in an elementary music classroom. They still think all the kids do is sit around and sing songs from a textbook for 45 minutes. But, as you know it's so much more than that. Not only are the kids doing so much music learning, they also learn it in a variety of different ways, integrate music with different subject areas, and use various learning styles.

Advocate for your music program during everyday conversations with the other teachers too. Tell them about what's going on in the music room, the lightbulb moment you saw from one of their students, and what you plan to do in the coming months. Once others see how much you value music, it will begin to make sense. They will in turn advocate FOR you. These parents, teachers, and administrators will show up when there are budget cuts to advocate for your position. They'll tell of the success stories of their children, about how music changed the lives of the kids at your school, and how valued you and what you bring to the world of education truly is.

Conclusion

Although there's so much you didn't learn in college about being an elementary music teacher, my goal with this book is for you to make forward motion whether you're brand new to teaching or are in year 25. Take what you've read and apply it to your teaching situation. Process through your thoughts and write down ideas you can begin implementing with your students and in your classroom.

Remember, you are a unique person and teacher with your own teaching style and personality. The way you do things won't look like anyone else. That's what makes you YOU! Think about your students and what they need from you. What do you need to change moving forward? Are there certain tweaks in your teaching or classroom that need to be done? Are there conversations with colleagues that need to be had? Do you need to prioritize your time a bit better between home and school?

Answer these questions and then make an action plan to move forward with success. Don't stay stuck, but take things one day, week, or month at a time. You have what it takes to be a fantastic music teacher. Please don't doubt your calling even for one second. Your students need the exact music teacher that you are and not the one down the street. Go into your music classroom with confidence, knowing you have what it takes. Also, remember to give yourself grace and patience as you grow into the teacher you're wanting to be.

So, how can you move forward from here? Connect with other music teachers online or in person. Find those teachers you can rely on for support all school year long. Let them come beside you and listen to advice and learn from them. Don't do teaching alone. Get off of that music teacher island, and allow others to come along beside you to lift you up when you're needing the most support.

Then, let's keep the conversation going online. First, come check out my website at www.thedomesticmusician.com to see the latest podcast episodes and free resources. Then, become a TDM insider. After you join The Domestic Musician email list at subscribepage.com/makeanote, you'll be updated about the latest podcast episodes, given tons of music teacher support throughout the school year, and will feel completely loved-on as a music teacher.

Join the Elementary Music Teacher Community Facebook group at facebook.com/groups/elementarymusicteachercommunity where we'll continue talking about the topics in this book in upcoming challenges together.

Made in the USA
Columbia, SC
22 December 2022

73687053R00076